Life Cycle of a

Salmon

Angela Royston

Heinemann
LIBRARY

For more information about Heinemann Library books, or to order, please telephone +44 (0)1865 888066, or send a fax to +44 (0)1865 314091. You can visit our web site at www.heinemann.co.uk

First published in Great Britain by Heinemann Library,
Halley Court, Jordan Hill, Oxford OX2 8EJ
a division of Reed Educational and Professional Publishing Ltd.
Heinemann is a registered trademark of Reed Educational & Professional Publishing Ltd.

OXFORD   MELBOURNE   AUCKLAND
JOHANNESBURG   BLANTYRE   GABORONE
IBADAN   PORTSMOUTH (NH) USA   CHICAGO

Designed by Celia Floyd
Illustrations by Alan Fraser
Printed in China by South China Printing Co. Ltd.

04 03 02 01 00
10 9 8 7 6 5 4 3 2 1

ISBN 0 431 08390 8

British Library Cataloguing in Publication Data

Royston, Angela
  Life cycle of a salmon
  1. Salmon – Life cycles – Juvenile literature
  I. Title   II. Salmon
  597.5'6

Acknowledgements
The Publisher would like to thank the following for permission to reproduce photographs:

Ardea London: Francois Gohier p.19, Jean-Paul Ferrero p.4; Bruce Coleman Collection: Fred Bruemmer p.11, Jeff Foott p.5, p.24, p.25, Johnny Johnson p.21, Pacific Stock p.26; Catalogue 395: Natalie B Fobes p.10, p.12; Corbis: p.17, p.18, p.27; FLPA: D Maslowski p.14, Gerard Lacz p.15; Heather Angel: p.20; Oxford Scientific Films: Jeff Foott p.6, p.7, p.8, p.23, Martyn Chillmaid p.16; Planet Earth Pictures: Allan Parker p.13; Wildlife Matters: p.9, p.22.

Cover photograph reproduced with the permission of Corbis

Every effort has been made to contact copyright holders of any material reproduced in this book. Any omissions will be rectified in subsequent printings if notice is given to the Publisher.

Contents

What is a salmon?

A salmon is a fish. Some fish, such as these trout, live only in **freshwater** rivers or lakes. Other kinds of fish live only in the **saltwater** of the sea.

Egg hatching

4 months

1 year

Salmon are unusual because they live part of their lives in freshwater and part in the sea. This book is about the life of a sockeye salmon.

Fully grown

6 years

Mating

Eggs hatch out

In autumn, a **female** fish laid this nest of eggs. Some eggs have a new fish growing inside them.

Egg hatching   4 months   1 year

This tiny fish has just **hatched** from one of the eggs. The egg **yolk** is still joined to his stomach and will provide food for the young fish.

Fully grown

6 years

Mating

4 months old

The young fish has almost finished his store of food. He swims in the **freshwater** of the stream looking for insects and **plankton** to eat.

Egg hatching   4 months   1 year

The cold, mountain stream is home
to millions of young salmon **fry**.
Many of the fry are eaten by birds
and other fish.

Fully grown

6 years

Mating

1 year old

The young salmon are now as big as a human finger. They leave the stream and start the long journey to the sea to find new food and grow into adults.

Egg hatching

4 months

1 year

The stream becomes a river and
the river gets wider. The little fish
swim under logs and around boats.
Many die on the way.

Fully grown

6 years

Mating

2 weeks later

The water begins to smell salty and soon the river flows into the sea. The fish flicks his strong tail and pushes himself through the water.

Egg hatching

4 months

I year

New dangers await the fish in the sea. This tern has just caught a small fish to eat.

Fully grown

6 years

Mating

6 months later

The salmon swims north into the cold seas around Alaska. He finds plenty of food in these icy seas and grows bigger and stronger.

Egg hatching   4 months   1 year

This seal is hunting for fish to eat. The salmon is lucky. He is not caught by a seal, or by any other hungry animal.

Fully grown

6 years

Mating

3 years later

The salmon is swimming far out to sea into the deep **ocean** water. He feeds on shrimp, squid and small fish.

Egg hatching   4 months   I year

This fishing boat is also catching squid and tuna. Some salmon are caught in the fishing nets.

Fully grown

6 years

Mating

6 years old

The salmon is now fully grown. He finds his way back to the river he left five years before and swims back **upstream**.

Egg hatching

4 months

1 year

On his journey the salmon has to jump over waterfalls. He leaps into the air and flicks his tail. He keeps trying until he jumps right over.

Fully grown

6 years

Mating

3 weeks later

Many other salmon are swimming up the river too. They are now ready to **mate** and their skin changes colour to bright red as they swim **upstream**.

Egg hatching

4 months

1 year

The salmon do not eat during their
long journey, but this hungry bear
is about to eat one of them!

Fully grown

6 years

Mating

2 weeks later

By autumn the salmon has reached the mountain stream where he was born. Hundreds of other salmon have returned too.

Egg hatching   4 months   1 year

The **male** fish have sharp, black **snouts**. The **females** are fat with eggs. It is time to **mate**.

Fully grown   6 years   Mating

Mating

The **female** uses her tail to dig a nest in the gravel on the bed of the stream. She then lets the eggs fall from her body into the nest.

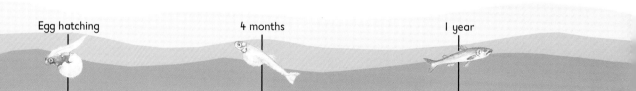

Egg hatching

4 months

1 year

The **male** swims after her and covers the eggs with his **sperm**. The female flicks more gravel over the nest to hide it.

Fully grown

6 years

Mating

Journey's end

The salmon's life is over. The fish are tired and weak after their long, difficult swim up the river. This bald eagle grabs one of them.

Egg hatching

4 months

1 year

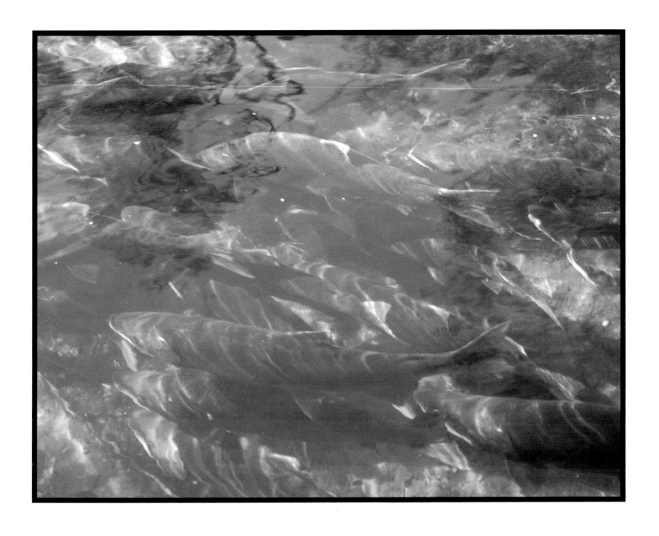

The rest die soon after their eggs are laid. In ten weeks time the eggs will **hatch** and thousands more tiny salmon will swim in the stream.

Fully grown

6 years

Mating

Life Cycle

Egg hatching

Four months old

10 months later

Fully grown

Mating

The end of the journey

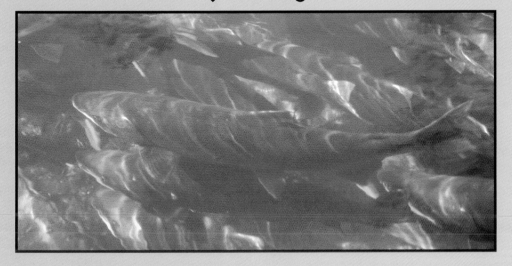

Fact file

There are seven different kinds of salmon. The sockeye and five other kinds live in the Pacific **Ocean** and just one kind lives in the Atlantic Ocean.

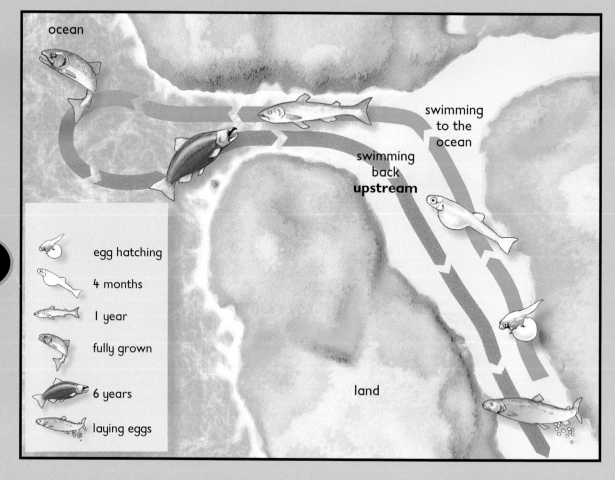

ocean

swimming to the ocean

swimming back **upstream**

land

egg hatching

4 months

1 year

fully grown

6 years

laying eggs

Glossary

female   girl

freshwater   water in streams, rivers and lakes that does not taste salty

fry   young salmon

hatch   break out of an egg

male   boy

mate   when a male and a female come together to make babies

ocean   the saltwater that covers most of the Earth's surface

plankton   very tiny plants and animals that live in water

saltwater   sea water contains salt which makes it taste salty

snout   the nose and mouth when both stick out together

sperm   this mixes with the eggs from the female to make new babies

upstream   against the flow of the water

yolk   store of food inside an egg

Index